20TH CENTURY MEDIA

1900-20

PRINT TO PICTURES

Please visit our web site at: www.garethstevens.com
For a free color catalog describing Gareth Stevens Publishing's
list of high-quality books and multimedia programs, call
1-800-542-2595 (USA) or 1-800-387-3178 (Canada).
Gareth Stevens Publishing's fax: (414) 332-3567.

Library of Congress Cataloging-in-Publication Data

Parker, Steve.
    20th century media / by Steve Parker.
        v. cm.
    Includes bibliographical references and index.
    Contents: [1] 1900–20: print to pictures.   [2] 20s & 30s: entertainment for all.
[3] 40s & 50s: power and persuasion.   [4] 1960s: the Satellite Age.   [5] 70s & 80s:
global technology.   [6] 1990s: electronic media.
    ISBN 0-8368-3182-9 (v. 1: lib. bdg.) — ISBN 0-8368-3183-7 (v. 2: lib. bdg.) —
ISBN 0-8368-3184-5 (v. 3: lib. bdg.) — ISBN 0-8368-3185-3 (v. 4: lib. bdg.) —
ISBN 0-8368-3186-1 (v. 5: lib. bdg.) — ISBN 0-8368-3187-X (v. 6: lib. bdg.)
    1. Mass media—History—20th century—Juvenile literature.   [1. Mass
media—History—20th century.]   I. Title: Twentieth century media.   II. Title.
P91.2.P37   2002
302.23'09'04—dc21   2002022556

This North American edition first published in 2002 by
Gareth Stevens Publishing
A World Almanac Education Group Company
330 West Olive Street, Suite 100
Milwaukee, Wisconsin 53212 USA

Original edition © 2002 by David West Children's Books. First published in Great Britain
in 2002 by Heinemann Library, Halley Court, Jordan Hill, Oxford OX2 8EJ, a division of Reed
Educational and Professional Publishing Limited. This U.S. edition © 2002 by Gareth Stevens, Inc.
Additional end matter © 2002 by Gareth Stevens, Inc.

Designer: Rob Shone
Editor: James Pickering
Picture Research: Carrie Haines

Gareth Stevens Editor: Dorothy L. Gibbs

Photo Credits:
Abbreviations: (t) top, (m) middle, (b) bottom, (l) left, (r) right

AKG: cover (bl), pages 6(l), 8-9, 9(t, br), 14(tr), 15(ml, b), 17(tr), 20(bl), 22-23, 23(tr), 26(tl, mr),
    28(tl), 29(tl).
The Art Archive/Ocean Memorabilia Collection: page 7(br); Dagli Orti: pages 16(tr), 25(bm).
Courtesy of the Clark Collection of the Smithsonian Institution and Dr. Frank R. Millikan: page 17(br).
The Culture Archive: page 13(mr).
Dover Books: pages 4(bl), 4-5(background), 12-13, 26(bm), 28-29.
Mary Evans Picture Library: cover (br), pages 3, 4(tr, mr), 4-5, 6(tr), 7(mr), 8(l), 9(mr), 10(both),
    11(br), 12(l), 13(bl, m), 14(bl), 15(tl), 16(bl), 18(l), 18-19(both), 19(both), 21(tl), 23(br), 24(b),
    27(tr), 28(br), 29(tr).
Hulton Archive: pages 5(r), 6-7, 11(bl), 12(r), 16-17, 21(mr), 29(br).
The Kobal Collection: pages 11(tr), 20(tr), 22(both).
Lebrecht Collection: cover (m), pages 5(t), 24(t), 25(tr, bl).
Science & Society: page 27(bl).

Printed in the United States of America

1 2 3 4 5 6 7 8 9 06 05 04 03 02

20TH CENTURY MEDIA

MEDIA

1900-20

PRINT TO PICTURES

Steve Parker

Gareth Stevens Publishing
A WORLD ALMANAC EDUCATION GROUP COMPANY

CONTENTS

Before television or radio, newspapers were the main medium for finding out about local and world events.

Even a century ago, the media were invading people's private lives.

THE MASS MEDIA

Scientists discover a miracle drug. Thousands of people flee from an erupting volcano. A new singer tops the charts. We find out what is happening in the world through the media. We are entertained by the media, too. The media communicate news, information, and opinions, and the mass media reach millions.

Today's mass media include television, radio, newspapers, magazines, photographs and other images, music, movies, and, of course, computers linked to the Internet. At the beginning of the 20th century, however, mass media were very different. Television and the Internet, two of today's most popular mass media, did not exist. Nevertheless, the business of mass media was huge and powerful. Bosses raced to find better and faster media technologies to keep them one step ahead of their rivals.

"HIS MASTER'S VOICE"

Recorded sound was just beginning in the 1900s. Tapes, CDs, and MP3s are some of the more recent technologies that bring music and other sound recordings to mass audiences.

5

At the start of the 20th century, most private homes did not have telephones. Urgent messages were sent along telegraph wires, printed out as telegrams, and delivered by messengers.

The "moving pictures" of the cinema were only a few years old in 1900, but this new medium was quick to develop. It was used for news and information, as well as for entertainment.

READ ALL ABOUT IT

On April 16, 1912, newspapers informed the world of its most recent disaster. Only the day before, an "unsinkable" ship had sunk. On its first voyage, the ocean liner *Titanic* was crossing the Atlantic, from Southampton, England, to New York, when it hit an iceberg. The giant ship went down within three hours, taking more than 1,500 lives.

LA PERTE DU PLUS GRAND PAQUEBOT DU MONDE
Le "Titanic" a sombré après être entré en collision avec un iceberg

Concours du Supplément du PETIT JOURNAL N° 4

Although there were no photographs of Titanic's *collision with the iceberg, news artists and illustrators created images of the event using photos of the* Titanic *and plenty of imagination.*

RADIO SIGNALS

Some ships at that time, including *Titanic*, had radio equipment called "wireless telegraphy" that sent and received messages using Morse code. *Titanic* radioed distress signals after it hit the iceberg. Another ship, the *Californian*, was nearby, but its radio operator was off duty. Help was delayed many hours, which greatly increased the death toll. News of the disaster was relayed to both Europe and North America by radio, but there were no public radio broadcasts in 1912.

As relatives lined up at the offices of Titanic's *shipping company, the White Star Line, waiting for news about passengers and crew, journalists revealed an important piece of information. With its sixteen separate watertight compartments, the new ocean liner was supposed to be unsinkable, so it had only enough lifeboats for about half of the people on board.*

SHOCK AND HORROR

Information about the *Titanic* filtered through over hours and days, and newspapers reported it to the world. Each day, major newspapers printed several extra editions. As the death toll rose to 1,000, 1,100, 1,200, and higher, even experienced reporters struggled to find words to express the horror.

THE FACTS OF THE MATTER

Reporters, as well as shipping authorities, eager to make sure there were no cover-ups, investigated the *Titanic* disaster. They concluded that several key factors contributed to the great loss of life, which finally numbered about 1,510. *Titanic* was traveling too quickly in foggy conditions, its overconfident designers had not provided enough lifeboats, and help was too slow in arriving.

POSITIVE RESULTS

Long-distance air transportation had not yet begun in 1912, so ships were the main form of travel across oceans. To ensure that a shipwreck on the scale of the *Titanic*'s would not happen again, several newspapers started campaigns that led to reforms. These reforms included lifeboat space for everyone on board, a full-time radio watch while at sea, patrols for icebergs and other hazards, and the formation of the International Convention of Safety of Life at Sea.

After Titanic, radios were manned at all times.

The story of Titanic spread quickly around the world. Like so many other tragic events, the ship's sinking became the subject of plays, movies, and songs. This Yiddish song was published in 1918.

NEWS IN PRINT

In 1900, the main kinds of mass media were printed publications, such as newspapers, magazines, journals, and other periodicals. Broadcast media, such as television and radio, use radio waves to transmit information, but this kind of mass media was not in use until after 1920.

Printing presses were huge and noisy, needed constant care, and, too frequently, broke down. Engineers and mechanics were standing by at all times.

Printed news started with on-the-spot reporters. Street vendors were the final links in the long process.

INTO PRINT

Newspapers were in constant competition, each trying to get its reporters to the scene of an event first. Stories and photographs were sent by messenger or along telegraph wires to the newspaper's main office. A layout staff designed the pages, while compositors arranged, by hand or at large machines, tiny blocks of metal type to form the words.

OFFSET LITHOGRAPHY

Invented in 1904 by American printer Ira W. Rubel, offset lithography was one of several printing methods used early in the 1900s. In the letterpress method, image areas, or the areas to be printed, are raised above non-image areas. In lithography, the print and nonprint areas are level, but the image area has a texture that attracts ink. In offset lithography, the ink is offset, or transferred, to a "blanket" surface, to save wear on the original litho surface.

3. *Image areas on the print cylinder accept the ink; water-dampened non-image areas reject it.*

2. *Ink rollers put grease-based ink on the print cylinder.*

1. *Water rollers dampen non-image areas on the print cylinder.*

4. *The inked image is offset to a blanket cylinder.*

5. *The image prints from the blanket cylinder onto paper.*

For hand typesetting, tiny metal blocks, each with a letter, number, or symbol on it, were stored in cases. A compositor picked out and arranged the correct blocks to form words and lines of type. Automatic composing machines worked five times faster.

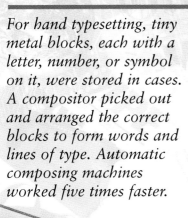

AUTOMATED TYPE

Hand typesetting was slow and laborious. In the 1880s, the process was automated by companies such as Monotype and Linotype. For automated typesetting, a compositor sat at the keyboard of a machine and typed the story. The machine selected and arranged small metal blocks with letters, numbers, spaces, and symbols on them.

The keyboard on a Monotype machine is used to set the type.

ROLL THE PRESSES

At this time, words and pictures to be printed were in the form of raised areas on a metal surface. On a printing press, ink was applied to the raised metal, which was then pressed against large sheets of paper rolling by. The sheets were cut into pages and collated, or put in the correct order. Horse-drawn carts and newly invented motorized trucks rushed the pages to shops and street corners to be handed out or sold.

STAYING A STEP AHEAD

Several versions, or editions, of a newspaper were produced through-out the day. Each edition had the very latest news. Because any delay meant that rival papers would be on the streets first, inventors worked on new ways to speed up the process. One new technology was called offset lithography.

This 1902 composing room served only one British city newspaper, the Sheffield Daily Telegraph.

THE PRESS BARONS

Even publishing several editions a day, newspapers cannot report all the news and views from around the world. They can print only a tiny amount of everything that happens. Furthermore, newspaper editors and reporters choose which information we receive and how it is presented to us.

POWER AND INFLUENCE

A newspaper's editor controls the day-to-day production, choosing which stories go into the paper and which ones make the front page. The newspaper's owner also has a huge influence on the events covered and how they are reported. Read one newspaper, and a certain politician is doing well. Read another, and the same politician is a failure. Editors and owners shape the news and have enormous power over the public.

When it suited him, William Randolph Hearst (1863–1951) fiercely supported the rights of ordinary people.

Hearst built a newspaper empire. He and Joseph Pulitzer competed by publishing stories in a wild, sensational style called yellow journalism. Hearst tried to become president of the United States in 1904, and governor of New York in 1908 (left), but he failed.

STORY OF A NEWSPAPER TYCOON

The 1941 film *Citizen Kane*, directed by and starring Orson Welles, is viewed as one of the all-time great movies. It is the story of newspaper boss Charles Foster Kane, whose career was loosely based on the life of William Randolph Hearst. Events involving media, business, politics, love, fame, and fortune show how a media tycoon might use his tremendous power to make himself even more successful, reporting favorably on his own business affairs and political views. When Kane is told that his newspapers report trivial events that are not real news, he replies, "Make the headlines big enough, and they become news!"

Actor Orson Welles, as Charles Kane, makes a political speech.

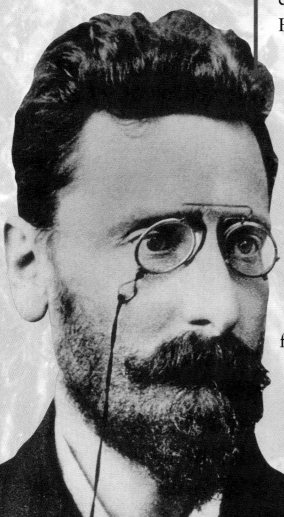

Joseph Pulitzer (1847–1911) began his career as a journalist in St. Louis. After becoming a newspaper owner, he added sports, cartoons, and fashion to "hard news." Pulitzer was also active in politics, and his name lives on in the yearly Pulitzer Prize for American journalism.

THE TYCOONS

In the early 1900s, many men rose to power through their newspapers. With his New York City paper, *The World*, Joseph Pulitzer helped develop the style of modern newspapers. His fierce rival was William Randolph Hearst, with his *New York Morning Journal*. At one point, Hearst controlled thirty-six newspapers. He also owned magazines, movie companies, and, later on, radio stations. In Britain, Alfred Harmsworth (later, Viscount Northcliffe) had a similar empire, which included London's *Daily Mirror* and *Daily Mail*.

FASTER NEWS

In 1907, Edward W. Scripps (1854–1926) founded the United Press Association, which used telegraphs and telephones to carry news faster. News services gathered information, then sold it as stories to newspapers.

Editors had to be available at all hours to evaluate big stories and receive hot news over the telephone.

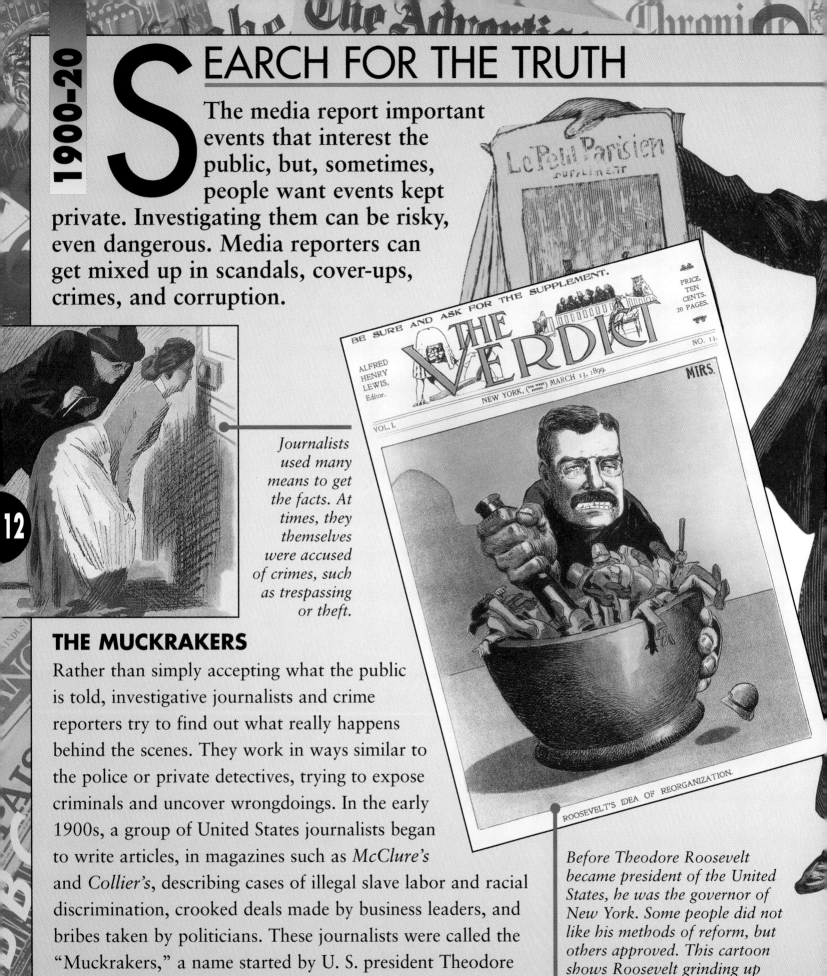

SEARCH FOR THE TRUTH

The media report important events that interest the public, but, sometimes, people want events kept private. Investigating them can be risky, even dangerous. Media reporters can get mixed up in scandals, cover-ups, crimes, and corruption.

Journalists used many means to get the facts. At times, they themselves were accused of crimes, such as trespassing or theft.

THE MUCKRAKERS

Rather than simply accepting what the public is told, investigative journalists and crime reporters try to find out what really happens behind the scenes. They work in ways similar to the police or private detectives, trying to expose criminals and uncover wrongdoings. In the early 1900s, a group of United States journalists began to write articles, in magazines such as *McClure's* and *Collier's*, describing cases of illegal slave labor and racial discrimination, crooked deals made by business leaders, and bribes taken by politicians. These journalists were called the "Muckrakers," a name started by U. S. president Theodore Roosevelt in about 1906.

BE SURE AND ASK FOR THE SUPPLEMENT.

ALFRED HENRY LEWIS, Editor.

THE VERDICT

VOL. I.

NEW YORK, (FOR WEEK ENDING) MARCH 13, 1899.

NO. 13.

PRICE TEN CENTS. 20 PAGES.

MRS.

ROOSEVELT'S IDEA OF REORGANIZATION.

Before Theodore Roosevelt became president of the United States, he was the governor of New York. Some people did not like his methods of reform, but others approved. This cartoon shows Roosevelt grinding up politicians to get his own way.

EVENTS ABROAD

Along with investigative journalism, another trend in the 1900s was reporting more news from around the world. Getting that news became quicker and easier when reports and photographs could be sent along telegraph and telephone wires, rather than by messenger or postal service.

STORIES IN CARTOONS

Comic strips began as newspaper and magazine "extras" to help sales. From about 1900 on, they gained fame in their own right. Comic strips dealt with a variety of issues, from home life to world politics. R. F. Outcault's *The Yellow Kid* (1890s) was followed by George McManus's *Newlyweds* (1904) and *Bringing Up Father* (1913) and George Herriman's *Krazy Kat* (1911).

Papers that carried The Yellow Kid *became known as "yellow papers."*

This Italian newspaper shows an artist's view of battlefield horrors almost half a world away in the Russian-Japanese War.

This Danish cartoon from 1908 questions whether stories containing violence cause harm in real life. If so, should traditional fairy tales, such as Little Red Riding Hood, be banned?

BAD INFLUENCE

The media were sometimes accused of having harmful effects on the public, especially on children, when stories and comic strips showed weapons and violence. Did they encourage violence among readers? The arguments continue today.

NEWS ON THE WIRE

Since ancient times, words and pictures have been sent from one place to another in a physical form, usually on pieces of paper. Then came the telegraph, which sent words along wires, as electrical signals. The telephone went further still — to instant speech.

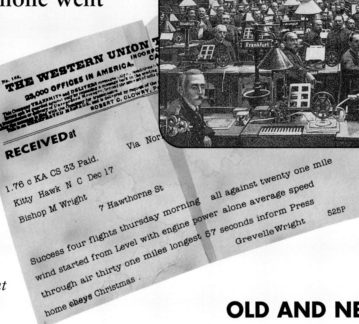

Telegraph signals traveled along wires called cables, so the messages themselves became known as "cables." A cable, or telegram, sent by the Wright Brothers to their father, in December 1903, announced a great moment in history — the very first airplane flights.

THE WESTERN UNION T

RECEIVED at

Via Nor

1.76 c KA CS 33 Paid.
Kitty Hawk N C Dec 17
Bishop M Wright
          7 Hawthorne St

Success four flights thursday morning all against twenty one mile wind started from Level with engine power alone average speed through air thirty one miles longest 57 seconds inform Press home ✝heys Christmas .

          Grevelle Wright   525P

Telegraph operators connected their hand-controlled machines into the fast-growing network of cabled communication.

14

PICTURES BY WIRE

In 1904, Johann Elster created the photoelectric cell. This device could detect shades of black and white in pictures and produce a pattern of electrical signals similar to the telegraph signals for letters and numbers sent in Morse code. Later that year, the first pictures were sent along telegraph wires in Germany.

A 1912 book shows how pictures are telegraphed.

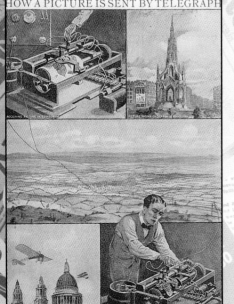

HOW A PICTURE IS SENT BY TELEGRAPH

OLD AND NEW

The telegraph had been around since the 1830s, when United States artist-inventor Samuel Morse devised a code of dashes and dots for letters and numbers. The dashes and dots were long and short electrical impulses. By 1900, automatic machines read this code, as holes in paper tape, at the rate of 400 words per minute. The multiplex system, invented in 1874 by Emile Baudot, used a very fast time-sharing process to send six messages along the same wire at the same time.

THE TELEPHONE

The telephone was invented in Boston, Massachusetts, in 1876, by Scottish-American speech expert Alexander Graham Bell. At first, this device was seen as a rival to the telegraph, but the telephone carried speech, while the telegraph sent written words and, later, pictures. Since each system had its own uses, they grew side by side for many years.

During the 1900s, Bell saw his invention become part of daily life.

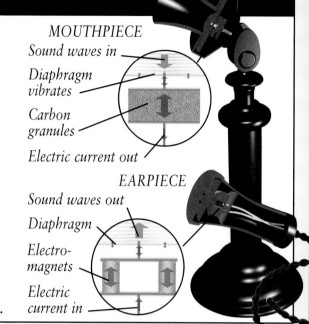

MOUTHPIECE
Sound waves in
Diaphragm vibrates
Carbon granules
Electric current out

EARPIECE
Sound waves out
Diaphragm
Electro-magnets
Electric current in

AT THE SPEED OF LIGHT

The telephone in the 1900s was spreading as rapidly as the telegraph. Both telegraph and telephone signals are electrical, and electricity travels at the speed of light, which can go around Earth seven times a second. This speed meant that news reports and other information could be sent long distances almost instantly — and needed no messengers. Journalists could dictate stories over the phone to their head offices, where the stories were typed and ready to print in minutes. More and more telegraphs and telephones, however, meant that streets were soon a maze of tall poles carrying hundreds and thousands of wires, each going to individual homes and offices.

Telegraph and telephone services were booming businesses. Networks of poles and wires spread through cities and towns and across the countryside.

In the 1910s, cities became choked with masts, poles, wires, and cables. This diagram from Germany (c. 1920) shows how wires could be put safely out of sight in underground tunnels or pipes. The wires joined up in a central building, the telephone exchange.

GOING WIRELESS

In the 1890s, Italian inventor Guglielmo Marconi developed an entirely new form of communication that used invisible waves passing through the air. Unlike the telegraph and the telephone, no wires linked sender and receiver. It became known as the "wireless."

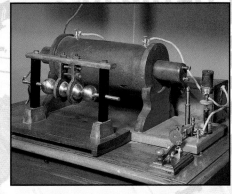

An early Marconi transmitter

Guglielmo Marconi (1874–1937) made his first radio equipment in 1895. He tested early versions in the attic of his family home near Bologna, Italy. Then he moved into the garden, so he could send the signals farther.

RADIO WAVES

The invisible waves were called Hertzian waves after the scientist, Heinrich Hertz, who first produced them in 1888. They are similar to light waves and travel at the same speed. We now call them radio waves, and Marconi called them radiotelegraphy waves. He used them to carry messages by sending them in on-off pulses similar to Morse code telegraph signals.

TELEGRAPH BY RADIO

Marconi's Wireless Telegraph Company was set up in 1900. Its first "wireless" systems copied the Morse-code method of the telegraph. Ships at sea were some of the earliest radio users, especially for sending emergency messages. Unlike telegraph users on land, ships could not be linked by wires. Early radio equipment did not send messages with voices or music, nor did it receive them. General radio broadcasts would not happen for several years.

ONE OF MARCONI'S EARLIEST EXPERIMENTS

ACROSS THE ATLANTIC

By 1898, Marconi, then based in London, had set up a network of radio masts around England. He reported on a yacht race in the Irish Sea by radiotelegraphy from a boat to nearby Kingstown. The news was sent on by telephone to the newspapers. In 1901, he sent radio signals across the Atlantic. This new way to send information across the globe became world news itself.

THE CRYSTAL SET

Signals to headphones

Cat's whisker

Crystal

CRYSTAL REC

Radio signals from aerial

Tuning dial

Aerial coil of wire

Radio receivers called crystal sets had no batteries or electricity supply. They used the energy in radio waves for power. Diode vacuum tubes were important parts of these simple receivers. Diodes were adapted for radio use in 1900 by Karl Braun, a German physicist, from his earlier studies of crystals. A crystal set picked up radio waves in a long wire called the aerial. Another wire, the cat's whisker, was adjusted to tune in different programs. Crystal set radios did not have loudspeakers. The radio waves powered very small headphones, so only one or two people at a time could listen.

Karl Braun (1850–1918) shared a Nobel Prize in 1909 with Marconi.

In 1907, United States scientist Lee De Forest (1873–1961) invented the triode valve, which boosted, or amplified, radio signals.

METHOD TO MEDIUM

Radio started as a specialized way to send messages, such as news reports, by Morse code. During the early years, many scientists worked to make radio equipment smaller, lighter, and more powerful. Then, in 1906, radio operators on ships in the North Atlantic were startled to hear a human voice, rather than beeps of code, coming out of their radio sets. Radio was developing into a medium of its own, for both news and entertainment.

On December 24, 1906, Reginald Fessenden sent out the first radio signals to carry voice sounds and music. The voice was his. The music was Handel's.

ON THE RADIO

Radio in the early 1900s was very new technology. The equipment was big, expensive, difficult to operate, and not very reliable. Messages were sent in blips of Morse code.

SPECIAL USES

At first, radio had only specialized uses, for police and other emergency services, the armed forces, ships, and airplanes. News organizations and the newspapers, however, quickly took it up because it made the reporting of events so much faster. Gradually, the general public began to use radio, but it was still an enthusiast's hobby. Most messages were sent by Morse code or a similar coding system.

Le Petit Journal

ARRESTATION DU DOCTEUR CRIPPEN ET DE MISS LE NEVE SUR LE PONT DU «MONTROSE»

A radio message alerted the Montrose *that Dr. Crippen was trying to escape after murdering his wife.*

RADIO "FIRSTS"

With the first messages to carry speech and music, sent in 1906, more people were able to understand and use radio. They could receive news announcements quickly and enjoy listening to music. Recordings of music on disks were still very rare and expensive. One of the earliest news events to spread quickly by radio was the death of Britain's King Edward VII, in 1910. Also in 1910, Dr. Peter Hawley Harvey Crippen became the first criminal caught by radio. He was arrested in the Atlantic on the ocean liner *Montrose*.

A family in England listens to a concert from Holland, 185 miles (300 kilometers) away.

BANNED, THEN UNBANNED

In 1912, new international laws said that all large ships should have radios for use in emergencies. This law did not stop the *Titanic* from sinking that same year, but, even though assistance came late, radio messages did help lessen the tragedy. When World War I (1914–1918) broke out, the use of radio was banned in many countries. The armed forces did not want public broadcasts to interfere with their secret "wireless" messages. After the war ended, the bans were gradually lifted. By about 1920, radio was ready for huge expansion. Marconi set up early public broadcasting stations at East Pittsburgh in the United States and near Chelmsford, England.

By 1920, radio was establishing itself as an exciting new medium, and a new type of shop sprung up in almost every town.

By about 1910, radios were small enough to carry in cars, to use in the event of a breakdown. In-car transmitter-receivers were an early form of today's mobile phone.

NEW TECHNOLOGY
After Marconi's early radio work, many other scientists improved the "wireless." Canadian inventor-physicist Reginald Fessenden (1866–1932) created a better type of receiver and developed better oscillators, which made electric current in a transmitter aerial reverse very quickly to produce radio waves. In 1918, with his superheterodyne circuit, U. S. inventor Edwin Armstrong (1890–1954) made tuning into different broadcasts much easier. Clustering around the crackling "wireless" was a new family pastime.

Marconi helped improve radio sets during World War I, demonstrating the importance of radio in battle. Before this time, messages were carried by riders on horseback, motorcycles and bicycles, planes, and even pigeons!

A MOVING IMAGE

The first moving picture show was in Paris in 1895. The films were made by the Lumière brothers, who also invented the equipment to run them. By 1900, "movies" had caught on in a big way.

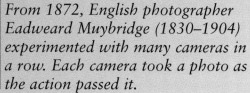

From 1872, English photographer Eadweard Muybridge (1830–1904) experimented with many cameras in a row. Each camera took a photo as the action passed it.

The Lumière brothers made more than 1,600 films. In one of the first, a train comes toward the screen. Not sure if the train was real, some viewers ran away in terror!

20

THE BIG SCREEN

Before 1900, people went to live performances at theaters and concert halls for entertainment. The Lumière brothers, Auguste (1862–1954) and Louis (1864–1948), changed this.

In 1894, inspired by Thomas Edison's kinetoscope, they began work on the Cinématographe. It was a movie camera that could take many still photos per second. It was also a projector to show the photos on a large screen to many viewers at the same time.

The Lumières made their first films in France, in 1895. Within ten years, motion pictures were a major new medium and art form.

CINÉMATOGRAPHE LUMIÈRE

Teasing the Gardener *was the Lumières' first comedy film. As a boy stands on a garden hose, the gardener looks into the hose. The boy steps off and — SQUIRT!*

IMMEDIATE SUCCESS

The Cinématographe and its big-screen pictures were an instant sensation. Within a year or two, motion picture theaters, called cinemas, were opening in many cities. Early films were mostly scenes from real life, changed slightly, perhaps, to make them funny or sad. Magician Georges Méliès was a pioneer in the use of special effects. As in *A Trip to the Moon* (1902), he created film "magic" by stopping the camera, adding or taking away objects, and starting again.

BIRTH OF A BUSINESS

Once a live performance was captured on film, it could be shown almost anywhere, time and time again. The amazing growth of motion pictures as a new medium worried actors, singers, musicians, and other performers. They thought films might put them out of work. In some cases, especially in variety theater, they did, but many performers found blossoming careers and even greater fame in the movie business.

THE KINETOSCOPE

Edison's kinetoscope showed 15-second films of daily life. Edison thought that films would not appeal to the public. He did not get involved in the movie business until others had become successful.

A kinetograph is the camera for a kinetoscope.

21

CINE CAMERA

By letting light shine on a strip of photographic celluloid, a cine camera exposes film and forms a series of still photos in quick succession. When these photos, called frames, are shown on a screen, the viewer's eye blurs them together to give the impression of continuous motion.

Unexposed film

Shutter   *Gate*

Lens

Exposed film

As a revolving shutter lets in light to the film through a gate, a claw moves back. As the shutter cuts off the light, the claw pokes into a hole along the edge of the filmstrip and moves the film down one frame. The shutter turns again to let light in on the next frame.

SILENT MOVIES

A book that simply describes a person's daily life would not be very popular. The first movies were like that, but filmmakers soon began to write exciting plots and weave together action-packed scenes in exotic places to create gripping new adventure stories.

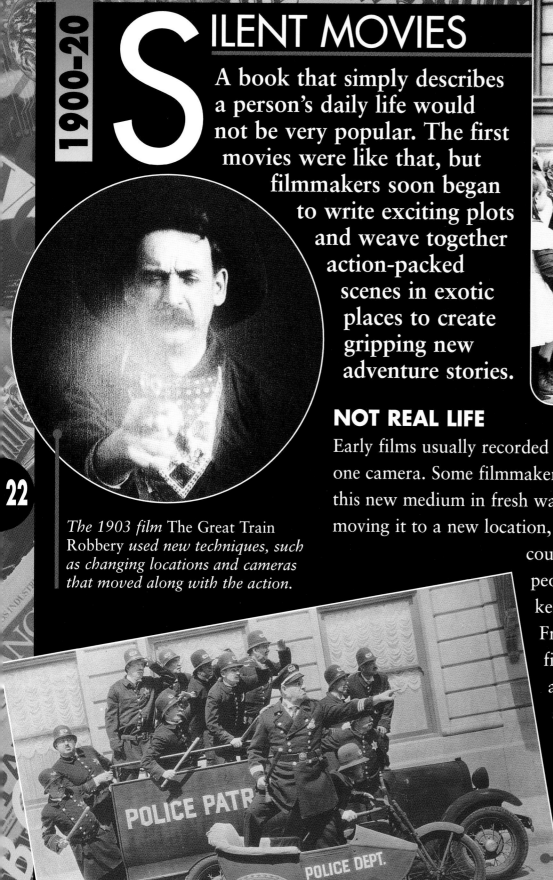

The 1903 film The Great Train Robbery *used new techniques, such as changing locations and cameras that moved along with the action.*

NOT REAL LIFE

Early films usually recorded one scene in one place, using one camera. Some filmmakers, however, wanted to use this new medium in fresh ways. By stopping the camera, moving it to a new location, and starting it again, they could cut boring parts, such as people just walking along, and keep the story's action going. From about 1900, many new filming methods developed, and different styles of movies appeared, from historical epics to comedies to crime dramas and thrillers. Especially in France and the United States, cinemas thrived.

Irish-Canadian filmmaker Mack Sennett (1884–1960) developed slapstick humor, madcap chases, and chaotic accidents in his Keystone Kops movies.

22

Films made specially for children were shown during the day, at matinees, while parents were at work or resting.

SMALL BEGINNINGS

At first, variety theaters showed short movies between live acts. Beginning in about 1905, movies moved into small cinema houses called "nickelodeons," which were often converted main-street stores. In the United States, nickelodeons held up to 200 people and showed about six 10-minute films, including a comedy, an adventure, and a newsreel.

MAJOR ART

Filmmakers, however, wanted to produce longer, more ambitious movies. In 1915, D. W. Griffith's (1875–1948) three-hour epic *The Birth of a Nation* told the story of the American Civil War and its aftermath. As movies became art, film stars such as Rudolph Valentino and Mary Pickford became household names.

In the mid-1910s, film's best-known face was probably Charlie Chaplin's. Chaplin (1889–1977) wrote, directed, and starred in many blockbuster movies of the time.

23

NEWS AT THE CINEMA

Movies were used to inform, as well as to entertain. At a time when many people could not read newspapers, and there was little radio and no television, films called newsreels showed recent events and were a major news medium. In 1896, French businessman Charles Pathé started a film company that became the world's biggest until about 1915. From 1908, his Pathé-Journal newsreels showed current events from around the world.

Audiences watched newsreels of World War I battles.

INTRODUCING THE "TANKS" TO LONDONERS
THE BATTLE OF THE ANCRE—AT THE SCALA THEATRE

STORING SOUND

Founded in 1901, the Victor Talking Machine Company started the mass-production sound recording industry in the United States. It manufactured a device called a gramophone, invented by German-born engineer Emile Berliner (1851–1929), that played sounds recorded, or stored, in the form of a long, spiral groove in a flat, rotating disk.

Thomas Edison predicted that his phonograph would be used mainly as a "talking machine." It would record spoken letters and reports for writing down or typing later.

THE PHONOGRAPH

Using similar technology, the phonograph and the gramophone both gathered sound waves and turned them into vibrations that were stored as a wavy groove. For the phonograph, the groove went around a cylinder. Early versions made the groove in metal foil. In the 1880s, the groove was cut into hard wax. For a time, cylinders produced better sound quality than disks, but they wore out quickly, and making copies was very difficult. By the 1910s, however, cylinders were being abandoned in favor of disks.

This Edison phonograph played recorded sound stored on cylinders.

RIVAL SYSTEMS

Berliner's greatest rival in sound recording was Thomas Edison, who had invented the phonograph in 1877. Berliner developed the gramophone to improve the sound quality of the phonograph, as well as to make thousands of copies of sound recordings from one original, "master" disk. Its advancements gave the gramophone the edge over the phonograph. People started buying these new machines and disks in large numbers.

24

Berliner used shellac, a plasticlike substance produced by certain insects, to make disks. Each disk had a 12-inch (30.5-centimeter) diameter and stored up to five minutes of recorded sounds.

A NEW MEDIUM

Recorded sound was a novelty for many people. They were amazed to hear speech and music coming from a machine, rather than from live performers. Yet, like cinema, sound recording soon became art and a medium in its own right. Actors, singers, and musicians made recordings for Berliner's disks. Among the early voices were established concert performers such as Enrico Caruso, John McCormack, and Fyodor Chaliapin. By 1920, Bell Telephone Laboratories, in the United States, had begun to develop electrical versions of the system. A microphone picked up the sounds, and a loudspeaker played them back.

THE GRAMOPHONE

The gramophone was mechanical, needing no electricity. A funnel-shaped horn gathered sound waves, which vibrated a flexible, drumlike sheet called a diaphragm. The vibrations passed to a needlelike stylus, which cut a wavy groove in a master disk. Playback was the same process in reverse. A handle or clockwork motor turned the disk.

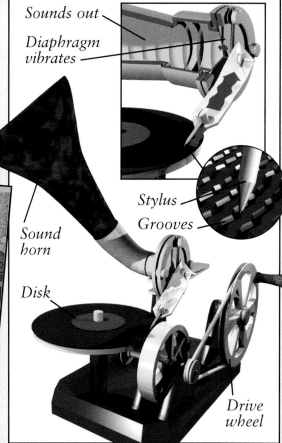

Sounds out

Diaphragm vibrates

Stylus

Grooves

Sound horn

Disk

Drive wheel

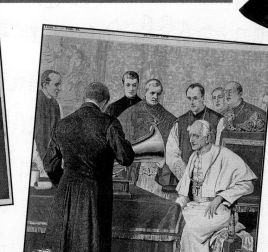

Italian opera singer Enrico Caruso (1873–1921) began making records in 1902. He became the world's first star of recorded sound.

DREAMS OF LONG AGO

COMPOSED BY
ENRICO CARUSO

Sung by CARUSO
on VICTOR RECORD
Nº 88376

OTHER SONGS
BY
CARUSO
With English and Italian Words

THE SONG OF SPITE
(Canzona a Dispietto)

OLDEN TIMES
(Tiempo Antico)

THE FORSAKEN WINDOW
(Fenesta Abbandunata)

ENGLISH VERSION
by
EARL CARROLL

LEO FEIST · NEW YORK

Many speeches were made into recordings, including one by the Pope in 1903.

PHOTOS GROW UP

This 1917 photo of American poet Ezra Pound is far from a simple, clear portrait. Taken by renowned master photographer Alvin Langdon Coburn (1882–1966), it uses multiple images and other artistic techniques to create interest and form its own impressions.

Photography became an important medium in the mid-19th century. Most photographs, from portraits of presidents and kings, to views of the countryside, to the terrible scenes of a battle, provided visual information about real life.

26

A NEW FORM OF ART

In about 1890, experts started to argue that this medium need not always record real life. It could be an art form. If painters and sculptors produced works of art from imagination, why not photographers? Photos could be valued for their own beauty and fascination, as well as for the feelings they aroused in viewers. The Photo-Secession began in New York, in 1902, to help make photography an accepted medium for art.

Lewis Hine (1874–1940) used photography for social change. His images of child workers show no obvious horror, but they aroused great sadness.

In 1900, Kodak's Box Brownie camera made photography available to everyone, not just to experts. More professional-looking folding bed cameras, such as The Ensign, were also mass-produced.

BEAUTY, NOT TRUTH

The leaders of the Photo-Secession, including Alfred Stieglitz, Edward Steichen, Gertrude Käsebier, and Clarence White, believed that photographs could simply be beautiful, rather than useful or true to life. They could be made with artistic techniques, such as combining images, altering light levels, or making parts of images blurred or hazy. In France, actor-artist-photographer Eugène Atget (1856–1927) developed a similar opinion. After taking many pictures of different, real-life scenes, he spent thirty years pursuing photography as art.

RECORDING REAL LIFE

Photojournalists continued to record scenes and events for newspapers and magazines. In the United States, Lewis Hine took pictures of child workers in factories. The tragic plight of young people working long hours for almost no pay aroused strong feelings and helped change society.

NO PRIVACY

As cameras became smaller and easier to use, photos could be taken almost anywhere. People of interest to the media were "snapped" not only in public life but also in private moments. Some of the rich and famous began to complain about media intrusion and the lack of privacy.

Invasion of private life (1908)

"Old Familiar Flowers" is an autochrome photo taken in 1919.

AUTOCHROME PHOTOGRAPHY

Color photography first became practical in 1907, when the Lumière brothers developed the autochrome process, which used filters to separate different colors of light. The resulting images had bright, but delicate, hues and a slightly patchy, or spotty, quality.

Orange grains — Violet grains — Green grains

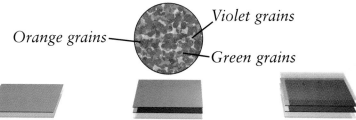

1. A glass plate is coated with adhesive to make it sticky.

2. Dyed transparent potato starch grains are added to filter out certain colors.

3. Varnish and a light-sensitive emulsion layer cover the grains.

AT WAR!

The media become extremely important during big events. In the early 1900s, World War I (1914–1918) was the biggest event of all. People wanted the latest information, and the news media had the power to change public views and shape national opinion.

Cartoons made feared enemies look ridiculous. Here, Britain's national character "John Bull" is being irritated by enemy "wasps" in the South African Boer War (1899–1902).

A TIME OF CONFLICT

There is so much news every day that it cannot fit into one newspaper. Someone must choose the news and the reports people will read. The news media should strive to report accurately, keeping events in proportion so that minor stories do not become huge headlines. When a country is at war, choosing news stories becomes extremely difficult. The government and the armed forces are involved. There are secrets to keep. Should media power help the war effort by whipping up national support? Although stories may contain accurate information, they might also make the enemy seem more evil than it is.

The Russian Revolution of 1917 saw the ruling czar and his family overthrown as ordinary working people took power.

This 1917 poster urged U. S. citizens to help the war effort by buying War Savings Stamps.

HELP STOP THIS

W.S.S.

BUY W.S.S.
& KEEP HIM OUT of AMERICA

War photographers risk their lives to supply news images. This camera is protected by an armored shield.

DIFFERENT VIEWS

World War I was a conflict so great that it involved all European nations and affected almost every country on Earth. Yet, the newspapers of countries on different sides might have been reporting different conflicts. Each had huge headlines for battles won but reported losses less fully. Readers on all sides were told they were fighting for a just cause. Not all sides could have been right. Only years later, when the full facts are known, if they ever are, can a balanced view emerge.

"OUTRAGE: INNOCENTS SLAUGHTERED AT SEA"

In May 1915, a German submarine torpedo sank the British ocean liner *Lusitania* in the West Atlantic. Germany justified the action, saying the ship carried war weapons and equipment. About 1,200 of the 1,900 people on board died. This event made huge headlines in the United States. Emphasizing that 128 Americans were among those lost, U. S. media helped swing public opinion in favor of joining the war against Germany. The United States entered the war in 1917.

The New York Herald *reported the* Lusitania *tragedy.*

THE NEW YORK HERALD

THE LUSITANIA IS SUNK;
1,000 PROBABLY ARE LOST

GERMANS TORPEDO THE GIANT STEAMSHIP AND SHE FOUNDERS EIGHT MILES FROM IRISH COAST

RESCUE VESSELS SPEED TO THE SCENE TO PICK UP SURVIVORS ONLY 500 ARE ACCOUNTED F

TIME LINE

	WORLD EVENTS	HEADLINES	MEDIA EVENTS	TECHNOLOGY	THE ARTS
1900	•China: Boxer Rebellion	•Boer War: siege of Mafeking relieved	•UK: C. Arthur Pearson founds Daily Express	•Marconi's Wireless Telegraphy Company	•Puccini: Tosca •Mahler: Fourth Symphony
1901	•U.S.: President McKinley shot	•Queen Victoria of Great Britain dies	•First cinema in UK opens	•Marconi sends radio signals across the Atlantic	•Anton Chekhov: The Three Sisters
1902	•South Africa: second Boer War ends	•Mt. Pelée erupts	•The Times begins its Literary Supplement	•First mass-produced sound recordings	•George Méliès: A Trip to the Moon
1903	•Canada and U.S. settle dispute over Alaska	•Wright brothers' first airplane flight	•UK: Daily Mirror founded	•Film editing introduced in The Great Train Robbery	•Photo-Secession publishes Camera Work journal
1904	•Japan and Russia at war (to 1905)	•U.S.: New York subway finally opens	•U.S.: W. R. Hearst tries to become president	•Diode tube invented •Offset lithography printing	•Joseph Conrad: Nostromo •Puccini: Madame Butterfly
1905	•Russia: first revolution	•Einstein's Relativity: public baffled!	•U.S.: first nickelodeon opens in Pittsburgh	•U.S.: first nickelodeon film theaters	•Richard Strauss: Salome
1906	•U.S.: San Francisco earthquake	•British Labour party founded	•"Muckraker" journalism rises to prominence	•Fessenden broadcasts voice and music by radio	•Schoenberg: First Chamber Symphony
1907	•New Zealand acquires Dominion status	• Lusitania makes first voyage	•United Press Association founded by E. W. Scripps	•Triode valve boosts radio and telegraph distances	•Picasso: first Cubist art Les Demoiselles d'Avignon
1908	•Austria annexes Bosnia-Herzegovina	•Germany: zeppelin disaster in Echterdingen	•Hearst tries to become governor of New York	•Safety film replaces flammable cellulose nitrate	•E. M. Forster: A Room with a View
1909	•Young Turks overthrow Turkish Sultan	•Louis Blériot flies across the English Channel	•NY Times publishes first movie review	•Marconi and Braun share Nobel Prize	•Paris: first appearance of Ballets Russes
1910	•Union of South Africa created	•UK: George V becomes King	•Dr. Crippen apprehended due to radio broadcast	•Neon tube developed	•Fanny Brice stars in the Ziegfeld Follies
1911	•Chinese revolution: emperor overthrown	•UK: suffragettes riot	•Joseph Pulitzer dies	•Rotogravure used in magazine photo production	•Krazy Kat cartoons begin
1912	•Balkan Wars (to 1913)	•Titanic sinks, more than 1,500 drown	•The Times prints its last Christmas Day issue	•Motorized movie camera	•Keystone Kops movies begin
1913	•King George of Greece assassinated	•India: Ghandi arrested	•U.S.: Indiana passes law to regulate cartoons	•Portable phonograph manufactured	•George Bernard Shaw: Pygmalion
1914	•World War I begins •Panama Canal opens	•Archduke Ferdinand assassinated in Sarajevo	•Cinema houses replace nickelodeons	•U.S.: first transcontinental telephone call	•Charlie Chaplin creates "Tramp" character
1915	•ANZAC troops slaughtered on Gallipoli	•Lusitania sunk by German torpedo	•Radio service connects U. S. and Japan	•U.S.: radio-telephone call from Virginia to Paris	•D. W. Griffith: The Birth of a Nation
1916	•Ireland: Easter Rising in Dublin	•Battle of the Somme trench warfare	•Carl Sandburg wins first Pulitzer Prize	•Radios get tuners	•Franz Kafka: Metamorphosis
1917	•Russian Revolution •U.S. enters World War I	•Spy Mata Hari executed by firing squad	•Uncle Sam poster recruits U. S. soldiers for WWI	•Photocomposition first used in printing	•Mary Pickford stars in Poor Little Rich Girl
1918	•World War I ends •UK: women get vote	•Armistice signed	•New York Times begins home delivery	•Superheterodyne circuit improves radio reception	•Virginia Woolf: Night and Day
1919	•Treaty of Versailles •Nazi Party founded	•Rutherford splits atom	•AT&T puts dial telephones in offices and homes	•First shortwave radio	•Bauhaus design school founded in Germany

GLOSSARY

amplified: made louder and more intense, often by increasing the strength of electrical currents.

compositor: a person who set, or "composed," type, either by hand or on a typesetting machine, into words and lines for printing.

diodes: electronic vacuum tubes with two electrodes, which were used in radio receivers to change alternating electrical current into direct current.

kinetoscope: a moving-picture machine through which a single viewer could watch a series of still pictures on a band of film that passed rapidly over a light, creating the illusion of motion.

lithography: the process of printing from a smooth surface, such as a metal plate, on which the image areas accept ink, while the blank areas do not.

media: all of the different means that are used to communicate news, information, and entertainment.

oscillators: electronic devices used in radio transmitters, which periodically reverse, or alternate, the amount or direction of electrical current to send out radio waves.

Photo-Secession: a New York organization, founded in 1902 by photographer Alfred Stieglitz, with the goal of advancing photography to a pictorial form of artistic expression.

telegraphy: the use of telegraph equipment to change letters, numbers, and symbols into coded electrical signals that can be sent along wires or cables to communicate messages.

triode valve: a three-electrode, electronic vacuum tube that strengthens weak electrical signals to control much larger electrical currents.

wireless: a system of radio-wave communication in which senders and receivers are not linked by wires.

MORE BOOKS TO READ

Charlie Chaplin: Genius of the Silent Screen. Ruth Turk (Lerner)

Extra! Extra! The Who, What, Where, When, and Why of Newspapers. Linda Granfield (Econo-Clad)

Film and Photography. Ian S. Graham (Raintree Steck-Vaughn)

Guglielmo Marconi: Radio Pioneer. Giants of Science (series). Beverley Birch (Blackbirch)

Joseph Pulitzer and the New York World. Makers of the Media (series). Nancy Whitelaw (Morgan Reynolds)

Newspapers: From Start to Finish. Mindi Rose Englart (Blackbirch)

Pictures, 1918. Jeanette Ingold (Econo-Clad)

The Printing Press: A Breakthrough in Communication. Point of Impact (series). Richard Tames (Heinemann Library)

The Titanic. Great Disasters: Reforms and Ramifications (series). Dan Harmon (Chelsea House)

William Randolph Hearst: Modern Media Tycoon. Nancy Frazier (Blackbirch)

WEB SITES

A History of Photography: from its beginnings till the 1920s. *www.rleggat.com/photohistory*

The History of Printing. *www.usink.com/history_printing.html*

Recording Technology History. *history.acusd.edu/gen/recording/notes.html*

R. F. Outcault, The Father of the American Sunday Comics. *www.neponset.com/yellowkid/history.htm*

Due to the dynamic nature of the Internet, some web sites stay current longer than others. To find additional web sites, use a reliable search engine with one or more of the following keywords: *autochrome, comics, gramophone, Lumière, Marconi, media, muckrakers, newspapers, photography, printing press, radio, Alfred Stieglitz,* and *telegraphy.*

INDEX